Thanks to Adam Funari for designing an
you to all who are close to me and hav
growing with me and inspired me to go after my dreams.

"We can never obtain peace in the outer world until we make peace with ourselves."

— Dalai Lama XIV

So, you are single again.

I would love to simply say to you, "Don't worry! In three weeks to six months you will be fine again, and things will go back to normal", but I know that won't work right now. The truth is, it absolutely will be fine, and in fact it already is fine. Look around you. The earth is still spinning. Everything that you rely on on a day to day basis is still existent. You are still breathing. You may not feel like you are breathing, or you may not even want to breathe right now, but do something for yourself this very second – be still, and remind yourself that you really truly are going to be just fine. This is the first and most important step in helping yourself to get over this heartbreak. You don't have to feel fine right this second, and I bet you aren't sure you even want to get past this, because moving on means letting go, but deep down, you and I both know that you absolutely, positively are going to recover, and feel happy and normal again.

Throughout the course of this book, I'm going to ask you to do some serious soul searching. I'm going to ask you why you two broke up. Why didn't it work, and what role did you play in it? There comes a time when a purging of negative emotions whether it is frustration, anger, heartache, guilt, or jealousy can be used as a tool to leave the past and move forward from here. These are just a few things you can expect from this book. What I ask from you, is that you immediately become aware and further commit that what you do within the course of this book is solely for you. In other words, commit to healing, growing, learning, and make these lessons purely for the "betterment" (if there is such a word) of you. Breaking up can leave one feeling less secure, and less confident in oneself. So promise yourself this: From this page forward, you are committed to taking care of <u>your</u> needs, and with every step you take, you will find one tiny piece of joy, because you did it all for <u>you</u>. It is so rewarding to do something for yourself, no matter how small, and to feel completely joyful for the gift you gave yourself.

Let's get started.

Who do you think you are ?

If you have read any of my other books, you will know I am a huge fan of keeping a journal. Not one that you type out, but one that requires a writing utensil and paper. This may seem like a pain in the butt right now (*can you remember when it was the norm?*), but focusing on your penmanship while you are generating complete thoughts into sentences is how you are going to go deep inside your body, mind, and soul, and dig into all crevices and cracks of your emotions and thoughts.

This journal is going to be for your eyes only. It's not to be written for anyone else to read at a later date, either. (Meaning, your ex – if you want to give it to your therapist, it probably isn't a bad idea) This journal will hold your truest and rawest thoughts, without pride, without ego, and without making yourself look like a victim. And, you will find one tiny piece of joy in this exercise, knowing that you are being completely and utterly truthful with yourself – whether you are right or wrong. Use your blank paper as a mirror and write down what you see in front of you.

So, for your first exercise, buy or get yourself a notebook or journal, and a great pen that you enjoy using. Personally, I find having that perfect pen just makes it a little bit more fun to write.. but that's just me. It's also something that gives me a little piece of joy.

When you are in a safe place without distraction (hopefully now or by this evening), I want you to start off writing about yourself. Who are you? Introduce yourself (yes, to you). Who do you THINK you are? When I ask who you 'think" you are, I mean, what's your perception of yourself? Are you a hardworking honest person who loves to laugh and take long walks on the beach? Are you the mother or father of a genius child? Are you the top salesperson at work? Does everyone like you, and can you get along well with others? Try to write a minimum of two paragraphs on yourself. This is not for me to read, nor for your ex to read. This is truly for your eyes only, and although I was being a little "dry" in my humor a moment ago, truly tell yourself who you think you are. Don't be shy.

Because I don't want you to begin reading the second exercise yet and have it in your head before you complete this first exercise, I am going to ask that you go no further in your reading until you have finished writing at least two paragraphs telling yourself who you think you are.

If you are like me, you will simply fall asleep as soon as you are done writing. Perhaps curiosity will get the best of you and you will write as fast as you can so you can find out what the next step is. I assure you it's nothing of eureka value, only something that entails more writing, and even better, more getting into your body, mind, and soul. Before you can grow, you've got to be able to know yourself. It takes patience, and a commitment to go through the suffering of "personal growth", but if you can apply finding pieces of joy in the process, it all becomes kind of cool to experience.

When you are done with telling yourself all about you, then please go on to the next page. For now, set this down until you are finished.

No, really…Who are you?

Ok, if you cheated, raise your hand!

If you actually raised your hand while reading this, I just laughed at you.

The second part of this exercise is to now write to yourself who you <u>really</u> are. In other words, are you secretly obsessive about facing all the soup cans in the same direction in the cupboard? Do you have panic attacks before facing others in a meeting? Do you talk about someone in a negative way because you see something in them that you dislike about yourself? Do you steal? Do you pretend to have everything together when you know you are falling apart inside? Do you resent your child(ren)? Are you depressive? Are you a liar? Are you still in love with yourself? Look at what you previously wrote and evaluate it. Were you completely honest about what you just wrote? Did you write about the surface you, or the inward you?

There are absolutely no right or wrong answers in this exercise. Something important to know and remember, is that the more awkward you feel, the more you are doing it right. Although I made jokes in the beginning – which hopefully you got – I want you to really go inside yourself and look hard. It should not be easy at first. It does get easier very quickly and naturally, however. Remember, also, that no one will be reading this but you, so perfect and complete honesty rules.

Try to write at least two paragraphs, but I think you can do a little better than that. If you want to start from childhood, that is fine. If you only want to speak of the last few years, then that's your choice too. Nothing is right or wrong – only that it is truthful.

Don't rush yourself. This is your time for you, and so find a little bit of joy in that moment. Even if you are bawling your eyes out because you just admitted to yourself that you kept someone from getting promoted at work because their religion is different from yours. You are not justifying your actions, but you should be proud of yourself for admitting some things to yourself you may not have been able to in the past. This is how you recognize things in your life that have held you back, this is how you will grow.

Now is the opportunity for you to drop all of your shyness. Strip yourself down to your bare soul and take a realistic look in the mirror. Is most everything you do really for the good of others? Do you only care about your own needs? There is no judgment here. Only honesty. No one will know what you are putting down, only you, and you must give yourself complete permission to be open and honest with yourself.   As I said earlier, if you feel a little discomfort, you are doing it right, and therefore, be proud of yourself. And by chance, if you are truly looking at your inner mirror and see absolutely nothing that is wrong, then you are one in a million and whoever left you is a true fool.

Write your paragraphs, and when you are done, go to the next section. Have fun!

Who do you wish to be?

So far, you have told yourself who you are, then told yourself who you really are. I hope you are not yet sick of your own company, because we are going a little further now. After taking a hard look at who you are, both good and undesirable, who is it that you really wish to be? I'm not talking about an actor or someone from history – but someone within yourself. What parts of you are you really thankful for? Where would you like to see more growth? What parts of you do you want to nurture and embrace? I am going to bet that some of you are looking at yourself and saying there isn't anything that you like. There isn't anything to make grow. I have to tell you, that is the biggest lie you can tell yourself, and here is why:

You took the time to do the exercises, even if you only mentally wrote things down. If you truly believe that nothing inside you is desirable, then you can identify with a great attribute called dignity. Yes, for there is honor and self-respect for any human to not make themselves look good in their own eyes because they cannot face looking at something less than appealing. So have a little pride in yourself if you cannot find something inside that you want to nurture and grow – especially, since this garden is for both weeding out old things and planting new seeds as well! Aha! Something to find joy in! And finally, if you truly feel there is nothing inside you that is worth anything, then you must now realize that that means that everything inside is worth growing.

Simply put, when you are down, where is the only place left to go?? (if you don't know that answer, then google it)

Instead of writing this down, close your eyes now, and focus on the parts of you that you really like. Think on things that you've done that have made you really proud of yourself. At the same time, take the things on your list that are not so desirable and mentally mark through them. Erase them, blacken them out, rip them away from the page. Wipe your slate clean, and place upon it only the things you love most about yourself. Feel the weight of ugly things drift away as light shines on your shoulders and mental slate in front of you.

If your slate is blank still, plant seeds of worthiness, and self-love. Self-love is easy to lose, but it is also easy to gain back. It only starts with the <u>desire</u> to love yourself. Let's make a garden.

Close your eyes for a moment and imagine a small empty garden in front of you. The soil is rich and dark, and the sun is shining warmly on its surface. The temperature is perfect. Kneel down along the edge of your garden and plant seeds of specific attributes of yourself you would like to see grow. If you already have parts of you that you care about so much, and you want to continue growing them, then plant the already flourished parts as well. Don't forget to add little signs so you know which ones are for joy, happiness, good deeds, hardworking, etc. Pull away any bit of weeds that have managed to find their way to the surface. This is your garden, so grow exactly what you want to grow, but do it for you and nobody else. Don't forget to add your seeds of self-love, for they must always be tended to.

After you have planted all the things in your garden you would like to see grow inside you, step away and be confident in the process that the sun, soil, and water has on your seed. Return daily, to keep away those pesky weeds that like to spring up and choke out what's valuable. Protect your garden. Protect yourself. Don't ever let the things that are underneath your garden destroy what is above the ground. In life, it can be drugs, alcohol, anger, rage, lack of self-control. Soon your growth will have withered away, while the weed flourishes in the very spot something beautiful was.

In case you are wondering what any of this has to do with getting over a break-up, the answer is simple. You are empty right now, am I right? You are in so much pain, you will do almost anything to stop it. Perhaps you want this person back even. The answer does not lie in getting this person back. It does not lie in making the pain go away, sleeping for days, drug and alcohol binging, sexual encounters, over working yourself, or signing up on a date site to meet other people. The answer lies in getting back to your own grass roots. Re-building your foundation of self-strength, self-love, and self-reliability so that you realize that you don't need another person to make you feel better. Feeling better lies within you. It's a journey that is fun and exciting to explore, and if you will commit right now to going through the pain of separation from this other person, and focus on places where you might have lost yourself, and where you want to be, you can rebuild your self-esteem, your inner strength, your mind's health, and who knows, with all this soul searching, you just might find yourself.

And so, back to your garden of which you have planted your seeds of which you wish to grow... Take charge of your emotions. Take charge of your life from this moment on. Did you know you really do have the power to decide how you want to feel today? Do you want to feel depressed over your love loss, or do you want find your own joy in growing yourself into the person you always wanted to be?

Don't worry if you can't even answer that yet. Heartbreak is a horrible situation to be in. Nothing feels right, and I know it is hard to find even an ounce in motivation. But you bought this book, and that is a sure sign that you are seeking to heal. That, my friend, is a joyful moment.

Who or what is holding you back?

Never mind any excuses or reasons you have for not achieving what you wanted to achieve. Whether it's been work, relationships, finance, education, the only thing standing in your way is YOU. Initially, I intended on writing a few pages on this, but I think it can be all summed up in just a few sentences.

No one stands in your way but you.

You chose the path you are on.

You decide where your path leads you now.

Be the change you want to be, and stop daydreaming about it. This book is designed to help you get over a heartbreak. I am guiding you to find your inner strength so that you ultimately take the power away from your ex, who has you grieving.

The love of your life has left you! You are empty and broken, and maybe even literally financially broke. So fucking what. How many times have you watched your friends go through the same thing and bounce back? Are you really any different from anyone else with a broken heart? Do you need to work a second or third job for a few months to get back in order financially? Now is the most perfect time to put your life in the order that you want it to be in. You have complete power to do so. If drugs and alcohol has gotten you into the situation you are in (alone, broke, and broken), then get into support groups. I know you know what I am talking about. This is the time to stop making excuses. There are no more excuses, and no reason good enough. You lost your home? I've lost plenty myself. You lost your car? Me too! I've even slept in my car enough times when I made bad decisions... but they were my bad decisions. I'm responsible for them. Not the person who promised to pay me for work I did, then didn't. Everything is just an excuse, and no reason is really good enough, because if you connect the dots backwards, and remain completely honest with yourself, somewhere along the line you made a wrong decision. Not wrong, but poor. Maybe that poor decision was simply beginning to date the person you are now grieving over. Anyway, think about it.

Now think about this: Your path is set out in front of you. It is clean. You may have a few hurdles, like finance, or legal, or employment, but these are things within your control. Take the steps needed to take care of yourself. Try not to engage in arguments, finger pointing, legal battles, whatever. You want your ex to see the new and improved you? Show him/her the part of you who is at peace. Do it for yourself, your kids, your sanity. It is much better to do the right thing today in order to prevent regret later.

What is your part in all this?

Ok, this is probably going to be the last writing part of this book. This exercise is going to allow you to purge all of the negativity and responsibility that you have in this whole mess. From here, we will be moving forward to the healing yourself part. Do not skip this last writing exercise, as it lays the foundation for which you will build yourself up in your garden.

The worst thing you can do is not take responsibility for your actions. Perhaps this is not the first time you have found yourself in this situation. I believe that when you become responsible and accountable for your actions, you can stop following the same patterns that lead you to the wrong relationships. Do you know why it is so easy to spot the faults in others? Because you relate to the actions or thoughts you have inside of yourself. It's a fact, there's no debate. It may be that you see yourself, or it may be that you see what you lack. Have you ever looked at your loved one and thought something really negative about them while they were doing something they really love? Why is that?

For this last writing part, I want you to write down your part in the ending of this relationship. Again, this is not an easy thing to do. Put away all the initial things that pop into your head about your ex and their part. Their part no longer matters. It's irrelevant, useless, and quite frankly, I don't give a rat's ass what they did to you because this is about you, and you need to find some peace (that's right, peace, not piece) of joy in this because you are doing something solely for you.

Did you lie, or refuse information? Did you cheat? Did you think you had something to gain socially/financially? Did you just pick the wrong person from the get-go because you rushed in and didn't do your homework first? Did you use this person to get out of a relationship with another person? Listen, if you did nothing but love this person through thick and thin, only to be left high and dry in the end, then let me tell ya, you need to be responsible for not looking at the red flags in the beginning, because I bet there were some.

DO NOT write about anyone else's actions but yours. Write it, claim it, own it, and love yourself for your own faults! I'm dead serious. You loved another for their faults, am I right? Love yourself for your faults, but first acknowledge them.

When you are in a safe place, and not rushed, write down how you contributed to the ending of this relationship. Be truthful, please. You would only be cheating yourself. Remember, do not write for anyone's eyes but yours. If you want to re-read any of the previous things you wrote down, it's a good idea, as it may bring back memories of events or situations you were in. After you are done with this exercise, you will not be reading it again, so please use this time to completely purge yourself of any guilt you might feel. This is designed to look at your actions, take ownership of them, and then later we will forgive ourselves, and find our joy.

"Your attachment to unhealthy people and bad habits, which offer you no real control, is why you're spiritually dying and living a life out of balance."

— Shannon L. Alder

It's all about you now!

Let's take a look back. So far you have taken a good look at yourself. You separated your actions from the actions of others, namely "you know who". That's a big step, and very important, because most of us can only judge the actions of others. Even as you read this book, I bet you are thinking about someone who should read these very words. It's human, it's normal, it's … well, it's <u>now</u> what separates you from repeating some same mistakes of the past, and moving you forward. It is all about YOU now! Truth is, it has been from the beginning of this book. We started with you. You identified yourself, your mistakes, your attributes, your self-awareness. Some things were not easy. Perhaps you feel some guilt now that you didn't expect. It's ok, because you are now at the part where you forgive.

Mmmm, *forgiveness*. What a healing word. We all want it from others, but how easily is it to forgive ourselves? Sometimes I confuse self-forgiveness with "forgetfulness". I don't want to look at certain things I've done that have hurt others or have been unfair, so I often find it easier to "forget" I did them, rather than acknowledge I did them and then forgive myself. Why should I forgive myself? Why should you? Why do you deserve it? The simple answer is this: You've heard it a million times, but here is a reminder- you cannot love someone else, until you love yourself. Personally, I once found that sentence a bunch of malarkey; Of course I can love someone else, no matter how I feel on the inside! Now look deeper. Are you loving them for them, or how they make you feel better? It's a hard line to figure out which side you are on. No worries, though, because this is the part where you renew or find your love for yourself, and then in the very likely event someone new comes along, you are in a much better place to offer yourself. But I challenge you with this: Love yourself, and see if you actually seek to find another relationship. Find another relationship, and notice whether you look for him/her to make you whole, or you look for them to compliment your completeness. Ahaaa.. Find the joy in that thought, and keep reading.

FORGIVENESS: As I was writing that word, I paused before I finished it, because I saw that I had written the word *forgiven*. Self-Forgiveness is as simple as that. Being forgiven. You don't necessarily stop feeling the parts that hurt, from your past actions, but you allow yourself the release of punishing yourself and replacing it with love. Just as you would someone else who hurt you so deeply, but asked you to forgive them. Your love for that person made it possible. You restored something between the two of you, and in the same way you will restore yourself on the inside. Have you ever asked God to forgive you, then felt that indescribable rush of peace and love course through your veins, bringing tears to your eyes? You knew you were forgiven and the slate was clean, right? Let yourself be forgiven now.

There are so many awesome quotes out there about loving oneself; about not letting others hurt you; about feeling whole again. Have you ever come up with your own great quote that should be shared with the world? How about one that you live by? Try to come up with one by the time you finish this book.

Now that you have taken a look at you, your actions, your thoughts, it's time to start healing yourself. In the following chapters, I will take you by the hand and lead you through some simple exercises to help motivate you each morning, and prepare you to fall asleep with lightness in your heart, and by setting goals, so that you can stay focused on moving on. These exercises are simple, maybe even silly at the surface level, but when you embrace doing the tiniest things for yourself, you can heal your own self by providing the bits of joy and peace that you need within. Let's do the first step – and by step, I mean literally!

SHOES: As soon as possible, like TODAY, I want you to buy yourself a new pair of shoes. Not just any ole pair, but a pair that you have been wanting for a long time but just never got them for whatever reason. Spend some time on this. These need to be shoes that you will wear regularly, like to work or school, for instance. I want them to be a pretty big part of your daily wardrobe. Wanna know why?

Think back on every pair of shoes you ever bought or received. I don't care whether it was work related, play related, or what – you loved putting on your brand new shoes and looking down at your feet throughout the day. You loved the way you walked in them, and you know you snuck as many peaks as you can anytime you passed your reflection, just to see you walk by.

So now, I want you to buy a very special pair for yourself, because getting up is hard enough right now. I know it's hard to wake up and remember that person is not there anymore. It's hard to go to work or school in the morning without the comfort of knowing you had someone in your life. He or she may have been the biggest pain in your ass, and maybe you even resented every waking moment with that person, but now that they are gone, it is completely normal to miss their presence. Remember, you are taking care of yourself now. You are giving yourself your own pieces of joy and peace. You are the means of your own motivation, and what a wonderful feeling it is to know you have the power inside you to do it! Buy yourself a fantastic pair of shoes that you can wear regularly, so that every morning as you are pulling yourself together to face the day, you can put on those fantastic shoes and feel good about getting dressed and moving forward with your day. I'm completely serious. (How many of you are humming, "These feet were made for walking..."?) I am...

The next thing I want you to get for yourself is **FLOWERS!** Yep, that's right, I said it. Order them or pick them out for yourself, but as soon as possible I want you to come home with or to a nice arrangement of something beautiful. I don't care if you are a man or a woman or a little bit of both – you are taking care of your own wounds, and if you have never done this for yourself before, it is not only fun, but you may even get a good laugh at yourself on how picky you are when it comes to picking out your own arrangement. Not only does this give you a dose of self-love, but it also gives you unexpected little lifts in the morning or evening when you pass by your very own picked out bunch of flowers.

Did we burn your journal yet? Unless you have a fireplace or a burn pit and know what you are doing, I don't mean literally burn your journal in an unsafe way, but for all illustrative purposes, let's get rid of that book of burdens today. Seriously. Don't go back and read what you wrote while you were digging into your lowest parts of you. Let it stay in the past, since living in the past does nothing but cause regrets, am I right? There is a saying: *If you are depressed you are living in the past. If you are full of anxiety, you are living in the future. The only way to feel joy is to live in the present.* ? Remember that saying when you do feel depressed, and see if you can identify why in the moment. You will be amazed at how quickly you can diffuse the negative feelings. As soon as you can, without looking back, **BURN YOUR JOURNAL.** Goodbye past, hello path set out before me...

3 DAY ME DAY. For three days in a row, I want you to depend solely on yourself for entertainment, relaxation, healing your mind, and cleansing your soul. This means no social media, no Instagram, no video games, or anything that does the entertainment work for you, for three days. Don't get cute right now and ask what about playing with your apps on your smart phone. Consider this a social media diet that is guaranteed to cleanse your energy and take you back to the foundation of your soul's core – you.

The thing is, you have everything you need inside you to heal yourself from this horrible situation you are in. You may not *want* to stop hurting even though you are looking at the door to the "other side" and know that it is unlocked. You may not have the energy to reach out and open that door. I hope somehow you have been able to identify within yourself what (if anything) is holding you back from moving forward. Is anything holding you back right now? Do you feel like you'd rather stay in the place you are at a little longer, rather than pick yourself up and even realize you don't have to keep feeling so sad? Identify inside yourself where you are right now. Did you already bust through that door and are looking around for the next step forward? What are you feeling? Know what you are feeling at all times. I've had times where I feel like I have the worst pit in my stomach, as though I've done something wrong, but I don't know why. A woman told me one time that the reason I feel depressed is because I am not doing what I should be doing. That was quite an open statement, but let me tell you, it got me to thinking. At the time I was in my mid twenty's and flunking out of college. Everything else in my life was going great! Money and work was incredible, I was in a fantastic relationship, I was doing things in my life that not everyone gets to do, yet I was simply ignoring one part of my responsibilities and though I didn't care, I guess I really did. Anyhoo, the point is, as soon as I made up my missed assignments and got back on track the blues lifted. But twenty years later, when I feel down out of the blue, I remember her words and examine myself more closely to see where I am being neglectful.

Ok, so back to Three Day Me Day… what did the world do before there was internet? Oh my gawwwwwd, how did we all survive? I used to read. I played tennis. I went to movies with friends. I wrote poems in trees, and made up stories and wrote for hours by hand. What did you used to do?

I'm not saying don't be social. I am saying fill your void with yourself. (I wrote a book on that too, if you need it) Take a walk by yourself. A good long one. Paint. Watercolor kits are cheap and great fun. Even if you don't know how to paint, make brush marks and play with color. That's art too, and it is very therapeutic to use painting to express your pain. Read. Even if it is something from your childhood, like Where the Wild Things Are, or Tales of Peter Rabbit. Have you read To Kill A Mockingbird? Take yourself to a simple healing place, if you need to. Go see a movie and eat lots of popcorn!

Whatever you do, do it for yourself. Plant some herbs. Fix your car. Volunteer at a pet shelter or in a food line for homeless people. (A great self-reward is helping others) Use these three days to cleanse your soul. That means whatever you need it to mean. I enjoy spending time in prayer. I enjoy listening to binaural beats and sounds that line up my chakra. I enjoy pretending to do yoga. (I suck at it, but I still try) Clean your home. If you've read any of my other books, you've heard all of these before. Cleaning your home has more than one vitamin in the mix. When you clean your area, you not only clean the outside, but you clean your inside too. Have you ever been cleaning and realize you are angry as a hornet, and have been replaying old conversations or past actions in your head from a time that wasn't so good? Instead of letting angry thoughts and actions fill your area while you are wiping it clean, project light energy and harmony as you wipe away and vacuum up dirt from where you have already been. Love yourself in the moment. Thank God for what you do have, and what you are about to receive. No matter what your beliefs (or lack of) are, none of us are designed to be puppets. We allow ourselves to become puppets when others decide how we should dress, act, or feel about something. Mahatma Gandhi said, "Nobody can hurt me without my permission." Without *my* permission. You don't need to become a stone. You don't need to harden your heart. You just need to be aware. When your mind is going crazy, re-playing scenes and conversations from your past relationship, and you are desperately in anguish, bring yourself into the present. I like to wiggle my toes in order to do that. Some are better with just a thought. My point is, get out of the past, and come to the current moment and stare *instead* down the path before you. What is ahead? Doing better at school or work? Promotion or graduation? Building your savings account? A new relationship is probably on the path too, but I sincerely encourage you to not even worry or concern yourself with that right now. Do you want to be one of those who uses one relationship to get over another? Trust me, it's only keeping yourself on the same crappy path that got you here to begin with, and I shouldn't even have to tell you that – we all know it instinctively. Don't be "that guy". Just know it's out there somewhere, and enjoy the thought of finding the right one, and then wait until you don't even feel like you need a relationship before you seek one out again. Hmmm. *Is that an oxymoron?*

So give yourself three days worth of doing things for yourself that fill this void you have going on right now. Not social media stuff, but stuff that you do for yourself. Go to a baseball game. Take a long drive in one direction. Take your pet to a park (btw if your pet is not used to exercising, please don't take it on a jog around the block with you, that isn't good for your pet). Take care of your yard, or clean your car out. Whatever you do, do it with the proper energy inside. Do things knowing you are taking care of your needs. I promise you, you will find a spark of joy inside as you do. So now what?

Get rid of emotional baggage

This one can be a toughie, and no doubt a long journey. Emotional baggage carries roots and definitions deeper and with different meanings for each person reading this. I will touch on a few surface points, but I will say that I am a huge huge fan of seeking professional help in the form of counseling, hypnotherapy, behavioral therapy, group therapy, you name it. If you have truly taken a good look at yourself throughout this process so far (or at another time), and know yourself well enough to know you have some things going on inside that could use some addressing, please take the next step in helping yourself and seek help from a professional. The last thing you want to do is repeat an old pattern and never really grow out of something that keeps you back. Maybe it has nothing to do with being broken hearted, but you've been able to bring to the surface something else. Don't hold yourself back out of fear or discomfort. Grow, and help others even.

Throughout our time together, you have taken a good look at yourself. You were made accountable for your part in the ending of this relationship. You practiced forgiveness. You spent some time with yourself. You are literally now looking down a clean path in front of you, probably with forks in the road, even. Which way will you go? Where does each path lead? The cool thing is, you get to decide where each path leads, really. I mean, you can sit back and wait for something to happen to decide which path you will go, but why wait? Why not use this opportunity to MAKE your future happen? I don't care how old or young you are. I did not learn to make my own future until I was in my 40's. Yes, I get pissed off at myself sometimes for that, but now I want to help others not make the same mistake. So, don't make the same mistake, ok?

Back to your baggage... we all have it, we've all seen it in others. None of us want ours. Nobody wants to take care of somebody else's. Not for very long anyway. So, how can you get rid of it?

"Out of clutter, find simplicity. From discord, find harmony. In the middle of difficulty lies opportunity." Albert Einstein

I have a personal rule I "usually" go by after a breakup, which has worked for me as a rule # 1: Do not date seriously for six months, and do not date anyone who has not been single for six months. I even go so far as to not make myself available for the first three months. It's not so hard – you probably aren't even emotionally available anyway, and this also prevents you from using someone else to get over the last person. I don't care if it's someone you've known forever, it's not the point. You aren't ready. You aren't ready. You aren't ready.

You aren't.

If you can't do it for yourself, then do it for the other person. Pfft... no, do it for yourself. A broken heart can be very attractive to a knight in shining armor, or to a woman who loves to nurture. Do it for yourself. If they are "the one", they will still be the one later, and not only will you see how self-sufficient you are, but they will love that part of you too.

Use this time to deal with the things that have come up for you. Depression. Anxiety. Loneliness?? Are you a victim of abuse? Do you have drug or alcohol issues? I've talked to many people with both who have no problem telling me they don't want help because they enjoy using. In as much as it is understandable to feel that way, that is the dumbest thing one can say to themselves. Go back to the part in this book where you wrote down things about yourself that you need to be accountable for, and dig deeper. Don't block yourself.

Do yourself a favor and take care of repeating patterns. Address that overbearing parent's voice inside you that kept you from growing in the way you should have. Find out why you keep choosing the same type of partner, or allow certain things to happen in a relationship. You know what you want, and you know why you aren't getting it. I can't tell you how to fix it, other than to seek professional help, but what I can provide is some co-actions to go along with this part of your healing process, so that while you are working on the inner, your outer self gets better too.

Building your own self armor

Now is the time to sculpt the layers that are going to be protecting the inside of you.

Love yourself more than someone else can. I don't mean being narcissistic. I don't mean being selfish or demanding that you get your way. That's just being a stupid baby and you're kind of an idiot for acting that way. I mean loving yourself in the way that you enjoy loving another. Remember how wonderful it is to take care of someone else's needs while they are sick, or perhaps starving at work and can't get away, so you bring them lunch? How hard is it to give yourself the same treatment? There are easy yet extremely self-rewarding ways to give yourself bits of joy just by feeding yourself something healthy for dinner. Reading this book is a way to treat yourself to healing. Make yourself a great song list and use it at the gym. You've loved giving someone you love your favorite song list, so why not make one for yourself? *Ok.. listen, about the song list thing, I have a rule about songs.* Right now every song on the radio is about you. They will take you as low as you want to go, and although it can feel soooo good to get that low, I suggest you go on a music diet that consists of bluegrass, Celtic, and classical. I know, this is not everyone's cup of tea, but TRUST ME. The last thing you want to hear right now is "You Were Meant for Me", by Jewel. Celtic music pulls from the earth's core and envelops your soul, and if there are lyrics, it's usually about someone stealing a potato and getting hung in the morning. Guess what – that has no relation to your current situation. If they are singing about heartbreak, it's usually difficult to understand the lyrics anyway, so swim in the fiddles and heal. I don't care if you've grown up on the hardest thug music there is, and that's all you like. Stay away from violence in songs also. You are just keeping yourself down. Remember you have the power to keep yourself back OR move forward. You are staring down your own trails. Which way will you go?

Join social groups. I love a site called meetup.com. It's not a dating site (stay away from those for now!!!), but an activity site that has something for everyone. If you want to hike or ski or play video games, it's there. If you want to cook or have mommy day or talk about computer programming, it's there. It is a fantastic and sure fire way to expand your social network, and you can even start your own group.

Read a book. Have I mentioned that already? Reading is for you. It doesn't benefit anyone else in the room.

Get a facial or have a spa day.

Make a list of things you want to accomplish and do the research on how to get them done.

Purge your emotions. You do need to grieve, but you don't want the grieving process to dictate your progress. Give yourself a time frame for grieving. If you need to be able to get up for work or school, schedule yourself a good hour to just sink as low as you need to go, and then again when you have time so it does not interfere with your responsibilities. If you feel suicidal, please contact a prevention help line right away. By right away, I mean put this down and call now: 1 (800) 273-8255. This is available 24 hours every day.

Celebrate your own life, instead of wallowing in the loss of someone else.

Forget thoughts of finding another person. You only need you.

Realize the little things that give you pieces of joy and make them part of your routine. It doesn't have to be the "forever routine", it is just the one to get you by for now. What you don't see right now is that by doing this, you are turning your personal fragile shell into a strong support that you can depend on. This is the story where Humpty Dumpty didn't count on all the king's men and put his own damn self back together, and got up and walked away. No one else can put you back together but yourself, don't you see? It's all in your power so wear your power like a robe and enjoy every wobbly step forward. Your heartbreak is genuine and I am so sorry you are in this situation. I used to let mine break me completely. I didn't want it any other way. If I didn't feel the hurt strongly enough, I would go so far as to self-destruct until I did. I needed to break in every way possible, thinking if I hit bottom, I would have a clean slate to climb back up with. What a bunch of crap! I am ashamed and I lost a lot of great opportunities, but it is never too late to learn, and I will never let that happen to me again. Neither will you.

This is the end of the book, but it is really the BEGINNING. Your beginning. Outside right now as I write this, it is snowing and I took a break to go and sweep the steps. It was a perfect powdery snow, dry and light. What an amazing world we live in. God is my source of love. Maybe you have your own, or don't believe in any god. If all else fails, try asking God to hold you tonight as you fall asleep. I did it in a time when I didn't believe in God, and I was instantly comforted as I fell asleep. Don't let what others say influence your beliefs or lack of. I cannot help but think that all religions came from the same source, but were somehow evolved into man's interpretation over time and thus war and such came to pass (we are, after all, human). Whatever the reason, there have been writings and prophesies of such all along, and for that I choose to believe in God, who says that all things are possible.

All things are possible.

From the author:

Thank you for reading my book. Heartbreak can be such a debilitating experience, yet it provides us with an opportunity to grow. Keep remembering to look ahead, and not in the past. Live in the present. Take care of your finances and protect them, for who can control you when you have all the means?

If you have purchased this book or borrowed it from someone via Amazon, please leave a review so that I can know if this book was able to help and perhaps others can benefit from your feedback.

Know in your soul that you are going to be truly ok. Be patient, and commit to going through the pains of healing, and give each experience meaning and worth. It is all worth it. Keep Growin! Peace to you!

Mandy O

Other books by Mandy O:

The Ladder: Getting over sexual abuse. Life starts today

The Ladder: Filling your void with yourself

The Ladder: A 5 day tool to help you while you are recovering from a broken heart

Written by Mandy Olivieri

Book Cover Design by Adam Funari

Printed in Great Britain
by Amazon